Dobroho vechora, ya z

Hello from Ukraine!

My diary is a real, ɩ
ordinary Ukrainian girl who, day after day, is
faced with military events on the territory of
her country.

My reality is the whistle of rockets over my
head, collapsing buildings and cities,
disappearing from the face of the earth, as a
result of the arrival of the "russian world".
We are getting used to living in the absence
of daily benefits - civilization - electricity,
water, heating, phone connection and
Internet; we exist in incredible tension 24/7,
expecting massive shelling, new victims and
new incidents.

During the 10 months of the war, we have
forgotten what a normal life is: how to fall
asleep peacefully in your bed, instead of
monitoring the news in the hallway or
basement all night; how to have a simple
warm breakfast, setting up for a new
working day, and not swallowing a cold
sandwich with water, without waiting for the
electricity to turn on; how to be able to
freely visit shops and pharmacies at any
convenient time, and not wait for the lights

to turn on and the opportunity to pay by card.

In this diary, I talk about my ordinary life, which is sometimes very similar to yours - I, like you, do everyday things, listen to music, watch movies, if the Internet appears, spend time with my friends and loved ones, learn something new, dream, but mostly my present is scenes of suspense from a horror movie - the growing tension before shelling or drone attacks, constant strong fear, explosions overhead and no hope for a better "tomorrow".

Now a little about me - my name is Anzhelika, I was born and raised in Donbass. After the beginning of hostilities in my homeland, I had moved to Kyiv, where I again faced the challenges of war, but this time even more terrifying, with full escalation. In my notes you will find out about how my worst day in my life went - the first day of the war, what happened inside the country, how it was felt and experienced by the most ordinary people, who firstly met such unbearably terrible events. How our life is forever divided into "before" and "after".

English is not my native language, I apologize for possible errors and inaccuracies in translation, but I tried to convey the content of my thoughts as clearly as possible. In the process of reading my notes, you will have a more complete picture of the events taking place in Ukraine, and in Kyiv in particular, you will find out about the peculiarities of the mentality of Ukrainians, our traditions and habits, and, of course, about my life, which I tell sincerely and truthfully, not ashamed of my emotions and actions.

I wish you exciting reading minutes and welcome!

P.S. I will be happy to answer your questions and read the comments.

Slava Ukraini!

Glory to Ukraine!

255 Day of War

November 5, 2022

One more evening without electricity. One of the most fascinating things is the game with card bots. I still feel the greatness of the unequal battle with artificial intelligence, but the degradation is going steadily. Do you know what the worst thing is when electricity, phone connection and Internet are completely cut off? Fear of being alone with yourself and your thoughts. And the all-consuming emptiness of your life.

Now everything seems unimportant, distant, and strange. Echoes from the seemingly bright and eventful life of your friends, acquaintances from social networks from other countries seem to be woven into an alien tangle of sorrows and joys, alien expectations and anticipations, leaving you in the shadows, far from the hustle and bustle of life. *Your only meaning is expectation.* I'm waiting for the end of the 8-month nightmare, waiting for a nuclear strike or waiting for death from anything - missiles, drones, shock waves, fire.

256 Day of War

November 6, 2022

Well… When you live during the war, from fear to utmost anger is only one step.

Electricity system here already ruined more than 40% and in Kyiv the situation is the worst. We haven't electricity 10-12 hours every day and with every next explosion it's increasing on 2-3 hours or more.

Every day is getting colder. People will be dying in winter. Massively. And no one cares. Like no cares about Iranian ballistic missiles, which soon can kill all of us as well. World is pretending to be with us. But the real thing is no one actually cares how many Ukrainians will be alive after this year or the next one. We are just a *platform for geopolitical ambitions*. And interesting, sometimes a little boring, reality show, which is going already 8 month.

257 Day of War

November 7, 2022

Today was characterized by significant calmness; the expected second day of missile attacks did not take place. Well, you also probably know that our not very ~~smart~~, absolutely stupid orc neighbors, have a lot of absurd biases and symbolic dates, like the constant Monday 'performances', that we have been watching for many weeks.

But it wasn't happen. So, this Tuesday was peaceful and almost normal. My daily wartime tradition is to get up and drive straight to McDonald's, where I can make a phone call and read today's news. Last time we haven't phone connection or Internet at all.

Our McDonald's is an incredible place during war, you can't even imagine, how many people work remotely: here and pretty 'modified' Avon beauty specialists conduct product reviews; and gloomy focused businesswomen/businessmen sell another Chinese flashlight, which, "for sure", will serve you for a hundred years; and excited students, who actively catch the waves of the Bitcoin and try to get, at least, a cent take profit.

By the way, it was hard not to try it by myself as well. An outstanding day to try to get back to trading ;) My last attempt was many years ago. A nervous and thankless topic, I'll tell you, but if you approach it methodically and professionally, there are still chances. So we expect good results (~~not in my style, but I hope for the best~~).

P.S.: Oh, and one more thing, I have a mini-holiday: _the evening passes without planned power outages_. I feel super excited :)

258 Day of War

November 8, 2022

We've been waiting for this for a long time. This is what we've been waiting for since the very end of the summer.

Hurray! The first step is done. russian's fascists once again make a _"gesture of goodwill"_ and officially _"transferred"_ to the other side of Kherson. This is what we've been waiting for :))

We can't trust the orcs, but the first step is done. The situation has reached a critical point, where it becomes impossible to hide it even from the untrained mind of the RU-mass. We expected it to happen sooner or later. And it finally started :) Then there will be more! And now we are celebrating another event - the elimination of the clown _Spermousov_ (from rus. – Стремоусов. It is how Ukrainians call him jokingly) - the so-called deputy of the so-called fake leadership of Kherson. (Yes, Spermousov was 'negative ressurected':))

As one of the russian propagandists said today: *"This is the last day of russian Kherson."* Let it be so! I celebrate these events with Sprite and delicious Ukrainian milk chocolate :)

P.S.: The day was very warm, such a pleasant spring weather. The blinding sun in the blue sky. And mysterious night with a full moon - windless and somewhere electrified. A great day for great events. Ukraine will win!

260 Day of War

November 10, 2022

Sometimes you see dreams so clear that the dream is perceived as a reality, a vividly experienced event. It doesn't make sense, but there is a feeling that the event took place and it is firmly woven into your nature.

My grandmother died exactly at the time when the military events in Ukraine began.

It was fast, it was shocking and unexpected. At that moment, everything around was perceived as an infinitely long and incredibly terrible dream.

Firstly the explosions at 6 am, then an eternity long road to the gas station (1 km drove 2 hours), fighter jets overhead, then endless sirens, air defense flashes and terrifying sounds. <u>A sudden shift into a hellish apocalyptic reality</u>.

Therefore, there was simply no time and opportunity to comprehend grandmother's death. There was no way to survive the pain, to say goodbye, to see her for the last time. There was only a misunderstanding of what was happening and a total lack of perception of reality.

The dream that haunts me in my mind is not something special: I *see* a slightly rejuvenated grandmother, without her usual crutch. Her movements are heavy, but at the same time it is clear that she is still full of strength and energy. Grandma greets me and my family with a smile. She bends down to whisper something to my mom with a smile. She looks pleased and a little proud.

Behind her stands a new single-storey house, it looks like it was built recently, not yet decorated from the outside, only stone blocks are visible, not painted and not lined with decorative elements. It looks big and spacious.

Ironically, she lost her own home during the outbreak of war in 2014. Massive Russian bombardments almost killed my mother in Donbass one February day and made a huge funnel in the yard. As a result, at the age of 78, my grandmother was forced to move to a completely foreign area, lost neighbors, friends and acquaintances (~~Goddamn you, russian fascists, I hate you~~).

A large number of exotic multicolored flowers grow near the house, which the grandmother proudly demonstrates and tells stories about how she planted and grew them. I see red gladioli shining through the window of her house.

"No, they're not real,"- Grandma smiles, - *"I just knitted it from wool yesterday."* There are several very well-fed cats walking near the house, one of which I managed to pet. Our perfect meeting is interrupted by the fact, that I discover that I have lost my

mobile phone; *and from that second the dream acquires the maximum realism of our everyday conversations.* ☺ <u>There are dreams that can't be forgotten. And this one is definitely one of them.</u>

Meanwhile, in reality, our valiant warriors have already cleared almost the entire territory of the Mykolaiv region and entered Kherson, according to orc media. Their *"negative expansion"* of territories in action :))

P.S.: The weather is cold and nasty, but the light was turned off for only 6 hours out of the usual 12. Therefore, a good mood has a place to be today :)

261 Day of War

November 11, 2022

Have you ever wondered what the hardest ordeal or experience you had to go through? The pain of separation? A sharp sense of disappointment? Loss of loved ones?

For me, this occasion was *the beginning of the war*. It united the forced separation from my dear people, and utmost fear, and absolute disappointment in a whole nation of russian fascists, among whom there were a large number of my friends and relatives. All of them have shown themselves as weak creatures whose can't help us and even defend their own rights.

From a dialogue with my russian best friend (ex-friend, already).

- *If you are called to fight with us in Ukraine, will you go?*

– *Yes. What else can I do? I have to go. But if something happens, I'll give the soldiers your phone number to help me get out of captivity.*

The war started for me not as unexpectedly as for others. I warned many of my friends that this would most likely happen, but even I could not fully believed in this cruel reality.

Earlier, in the morning on February 24, 2022.

Explosion. Windows are shaken. I'm jumping out of bed and looking at my watch: 05:42. I'm running up to the window, trying to see something without my lenses. It's dark outside, the lights aren't shining. But it seems as if everything is covered with dense smoke or thick fog. My heart is starting pounding wildly, but I'm trying to calm myself with the thought that a wheel has burst somewhere/an explosion from a gas leak.

Anything, but not the first thing that comes to my mind... I'm beginning to search news online. *Let it be just a local thing... Let it be...* The first message which I see now is from Mom: *"The war has begun..."*

This phrase is turning my world upside down. I can't understand it. Only in the sleepy consciousness the word *"war"* is beating again and again, the real meaning of the word is escaping. The body is moving faster than the brain is working in desperate attempts.

Get dressed, don't forget about the lenses. Look out the window again. Maybe I can see something? The darkness around abruptly is filling with lights. These are the same confused and scared people like me are waking up and starting to decide what to do.

Wild animal fear of leaving the house.

"But you need to go for gasoline. It's not far here, a couple of kilometers," – I'm persuading myself, not yet realizing that the panic has reached a critical maximum and the queue for gasoline has stretched just the same for these very couple of kilometers that I drive in 2 hours. Fighters are flying low overhead. Shock, I haven't seen this before.

Tension grow, when I see the consequences of the explosion - smoke from a burning building is spreading across the street from the residential complex - the russian world has begun its work to destroy Ukrainians.

The realization of *how* zombified this nation is comes only on a long road to the west - we drive for 18 hours with a constantly screaming cat. We hear explosions, automatic bursts, shots. We stuck, mostly not moving, in incredible traffic jams - but everyone is in gadgets, we listen and watch the news all the way, we try to digest what is happening. *A friend from orc-state (russia) at this time sends me a meme with a cat and asks why I don't react.*

"Do you even know what's going on right now? War began,"- I type, simultaneously

horrified that the bridge we drove over half an hour ago has just been bombed. *"I knew about the war. But why don't you like cats??"* Dialogues with other people of this country are beginning in the *same way*. God forgive me. Irritation, anger, misunderstanding haunt me all the way, replaced only by fear when I hear new unfamiliar sounds and see a terrifying thing which is flying in the sky: air defense knocks down orc missile, which exploded in the sky like mini-fireworks.

This is how one of the most difficult days in my life passes, without mentioning how my mother refuses to come with us at the last moment, staying to *fulfill her daughter's duty* - to help my grandmother, who was admitted to the hospital only the day before. *We understood that we could part with each other on that day forever.* Tears were rolling out of my eyes and it was a feeling of utter hopelessness.

And then we were waiting for the death of a loved one, hearing endless sirens and rushing in search of a safe place that did not exist, a cacophony of explosions from which you wake up in the morning and shake in the evenings, *8 months of constant monitoring of news, sleepless nights and long hopeless days.*

P.S.: Sad memories of the past should be mixed with something good. And I have the great news today! <u>Kherson is ours again.</u> We are insanely happy and it really inspiring. There is a feeling that the best days will come someday :)

P.S.S: without electricity for 10 hours.

262 Day of War

November 12, 2022

I was walking today with my mother in the autumn park and hearing nervous sounds of air alerts, which again rolled through all the cities of Ukraine. I was thinking about the nation and national identity.

Ironically, I have *completely russian roots*. I was born and lived for 20 years in a small town in Donbas; all my relatives are russian or russian speaking, my ex-colleagues, friends, and neighbors. And this country, where I came from, brought me so many difficult moments, worries, experiences more than any other. Speaking frankly: *orc-state has ruined my life and my plans for the future.*

Can I say like my mother: *"Yes, I am russian. So what? You can't throw words out of the song"?*

No, the very idea that I have something in common with orcs makes me *disgusted*. Fortunately, when I saw the Maydan with my own eyes and felt the unity and desire of their participants, I realized that I wanted *to be the same*. To be the person, who does not accept everything that the authorities dictate to her. *The person, who can change the world* and not only her own future.

Before I moved to Kyiv, *I had no idea,* how *different* our mentality is with the Central and Western parts of Ukraine.

On my way home to my native town Stakhanov, I lost consciousness on the bus and couldn't get up. But not a single person (and the transport was crowded) offered his help and give me a seat. Sidelong glances and shuffling - that's what always haunted me at such moments, instead of real help. In similar situations that I saw in Kyiv underground, mutual respect and help prevailed. Girls and boys were rushed to provide first aid, shared water and given a place to sit down.

You may say that these are single cases. But for 20 years, I have studied very well the *mentality of Donbass*, which is <u>close</u> to the *russian one*, where everyone spokes only for themselves and adhered to the principle of the well-known proverb: *"My home is far away – I don't care about anything"*.

That is why the same thing is happening in russian society right now - *war, mobilization, impoverishment, unemployment* - all this does not makes russians to stand up against their government, does not make them think that something is going wrong and they need to change it. *"As long as it doesn't concern me personally, I won't go. Yes, everything will be fine sometime and will be good as it was before."*

Meanwhile, the doors to *"how was before"* are closing more and more tightly, leaving behind the horizon the opportunity to speak out about anything (*Part 3 of Article 330.1 of the Criminal Code*) and even more - the opportunity to live in general (*partial mobilization? Oh yes, men will continue to be caught near their own homes and subways,*

*until your russian owner "Gospodin Huilo"
kills you one by one, and does not reach the
desired ambitious heights*).

Meanwhile, a large-scale air alarm sounds
for more than 1.5 hours and Poltava's
aviation goes to intercept another orc
missile. ~~Our brothers and sisters?~~ God forbid,
I don't want to have anything to do with it. I
choose to be Ukrainian, not the orc nation. *I
choose to be free, not a slave.*

P.S.: All day without electricity and heating.
Unfortunately, the end of these restrictions is
still very far away. Everything is just
beginning, thanks to our silent ~~"sisters"~~ and
~~"brothers".~~ But we will survive.

P.S.S: *Kim hinted at the complete liberation
of the Mykolaiv region. Welcome home, our
dears!*

263 Day of War

November 13, 2022

*Recently, there has been a feeling that the
end of the war will come after all. Not in 2-3
years, but pretty soon.* Waking up without
electricity and connection and falling asleep

from boredom and endless card games with bots, *only this thought* warms the soul.

Kherson seemed to be something unattainable, almost unreal. But the day of his release has come, and it has come much faster than our political experts claimed. What will be next? Melitopol? Crimea? Or maybe my *native occupied Luhansk region*? When we count not the hours of lack of electricity, but the rare moments of its presence, *hope is the most important thing,* which you have. And long painful reflections about what happened before. *I have no future*; the present time has been stolen; only reflections on the past remain.

There are no more regrets, but painful memories *"before"*. They can't calm down; they only show the gap between, what *was* and what *can't be returned*. Were my goals really meaningful? If yes, why is it so sadly for the time I have lost on them, when there were no precious minutes left for travel, pleasure, entertainment? *If I had known* that there would be a war this year, would something have changed in my life?

Questions, which are constantly spinning in my head and to which it is impossible to find an answer. But, with certainty, we can say that *I have broken down as a person*, who I have been building for so long and hard, there is no desire to do something anymore, to go forward at all. A feeling of illusory and unreality remained from the past life.

Our true reality now is *missiles flying overhead*; every day is like the last one, tomorrow may not come. When the lights turn off, the internal timer turns on, counting down the minutes and seconds of your life in your head. Moments turn into eternity, the inner emptiness absorbs and immobilizes. You don't want to get up, act. The only thought: *"What is all this for? What is this meaninglessness of being for?"* it does not get out of my head and hits the frantic alarm bell again and again. *Every minute*.

Many people ask me: *"What are your goals today? How do you live?"* Such a question can only be asked by a person who has never been inside this theater of the absurd. Guys, there are no goals, but one task is set - *survival*.

PS: *Today we bought the main survival products - canned food, stewed meat, dry food*. It's time to accept the fact that it's going to get harder every day. Winter will be difficult. We do not know where we will spend it and how, we have no plans for the future, only for today. And the only thing we can do today is not to let ourselves starve to death tomorrow. <u>My motto</u> for the next few weeks is: *"Prepare for the fact that tomorrow will only get worse."*

264 Day of War

November 14, 2022

Waking up every morning without electricity, connection and Internet, has become a *usual thing* for a week now. But *"usual"* doesn't mean comfortable and normal. Every hour before dawn, you wake up to check for bad news and air alarms (*especially on Mondays*). Oh, is there still Internet?! We live! Meanwhile, blackouts now occur at night, and the trend is growing every day. We are gradually preparing to enter winter mode :)

Meanwhile, the news background simply captures and twists into an uncontrolled whirlwind; you do not have time to read about one occasion - only the next hour it ceases to be relevant. *By the way, I am proud that Zelenskyy, as always, was not afraid to go to the frontline Kherson, and, meanwhile, putin didn't dare to go to the summit in Bali. But really, why should he dare? Every second person will have something to say there.*

At the same time, the *"second army of the world from the end"* - -<u>stole a raccoon </u>from Kherson. This may seem funny to everyone, except for the residents of Donbass...) *It has always been a very poor part* of the country. People from Donbass stole absolutely everything that can be imagined.

A child's bike? *Great, useful thing and my kids will enjoy it; we take it while that guy is picking his nose!* Washed to holes towels with stains? *Well, not the best gift in the world for my honey, but not bad at all, the main thing is that it's free.* We shoot from the balcony, doing acrobatic tricks while the neighbors sleep. Iron pillars? *Oh, yes, I'll rent it for scrap.* Crumpled cardboard boxes from the trash can? *Sure, it will be a necessary thing on the balcony.*

Anyone who has lived in Donbas will always understand that the fact that the orc army steals toilets and women's underwear <u>can't be untrue</u>. Donbass has the same mentality as orc-state. And this is a fact, these (*God forgive me*) people, are guided by poverty and the desire for easy profit. Otherwise, they would not have had to go to kill Ukrainians.

As a person who has lived in Donbas for more than 20 years and has spent quite a lot of time in Western Ukraine and these days lives in Central part, I would like to find positive aspects from my homeland. But, unfortunately, I don't see them from the word "*absolutely*". The human attitude is certainly one of the best in Western Ukraine.

Perhaps, this attitude towards me is observed due to the fact that I speak almost perfect Ukrainian with Galician accent, but that's how things are going there. It doesn't matter what language you use to address people, if you do it politely and adequately, you can get exactly the right response. The worst situation was observed in Eastern Ukraine, where I came from - people are initially aggressive and try, as in USSR time, to "*snatch something for themselves*", ignoring the rules of etiquette and moral principles.

P.S.: Meanwhile, I saw a juicy Persimmon in the ATB and couldn't resist. Life is so short and completely meaningless. A year ago, my grandmother was very fond of eating these fruits. *From life to death is only a moment. It doesn't matter, how long you live, 60-70-80 or even 100 years. It's just a drop in sea. Your personality will completely disappear before you can fully develop it.*

268 Day of War

November 18, 2022

I'm still feeling bad after what has *happened on Tuesday, November 15*. It was the biggest attack since the beginning of the war. The orc creatures launched <u>about 100 missiles and drones</u> at our peaceful cities in order to completely destroy the country's energy system, plunge us all into darkness, cold and leave us without water. By the way, *already on November 17*, the russian scum began their attempts to leave us without gas, methodically destroying gas distribution stations. So, our kind ~~"brothers"~~ ~~and~~ ~~"sisters"~~ are making attempts to completely destroy Ukrainians.

The memory of November 15th still makes me *shiver*. This is what keeps me up at night now and because of what I constantly wake up in a sweat. The first half of this day passed quite calmly. We had electricity almost all day. I worked slowly and thought about the long and good cleaning for once.

As soon as I decided to put on a heat-resistant sticker in front of the stove, *the announcements of air alarms began*. Zaporizhzhia, Donetsk, Kherson, Kiev, then Lviv, Ivano-Frankivsk, Rivne. Everything happened almost <u>instantly</u>. The work had to be postponed as soon as I heard 2 distant explosions. Such sounds were not particularly unexpected for me; I had often heard them before. For the residents of Kyiv, this has been normal for a long time.

But today it was a little stressful. The work had to be continued, because the lights could be turned off at any moment, so I reluctantly continued it, while constantly looking at the news feed.

The first rocket launch was carried out. And I got it not from the news but from the sounds around. How many missiles were launched in the first wave? 15? 20? We didn't know, we could only guess. Attack followed attack. Throughout the land. Every second. Numerous explosions in different parts of the country. Fear began to bind me and I felt sick from the tension.

Sounds began to be heard in Kyiv. Again. I only had time to read and count them. *Deaf and distant.* Then a little closer. The neighbors in Telegram are panicking. *Hit an apartment building.* And again. *The house is on fire.* One more. <u>Five-storey building!</u> There are people there, so many poor people! orcs, what are you doing?!

Feeling terrified when watching videos with the building. Feeling trapped. There is no way out. There is no end. There is only a count of explosions and an ongoing series of news: Lviv, Zhytomyr, Kharkiv, Ivano-Frankivsk, Kyiv again. There are many reports of flying missiles. *Infinitely long minutes that stretch into eternity.*

The second wave of missiles. Again. I find out about it when I'm going into the corridor. *Incredibly loud.* A sound wave rolls over the house. What's it? It's not the sound of an airplane, helicopter or missile. It's much scarier. *Windows are shaking.* Is the rocket going to explode now? The heart begins to beat in a desperate rhythm, as if trying to make up for the remaining time of life. My hands are shaking, my legs stop holding weight. Am I sitting or standing? *I don't remember, I don't know.*

Everything happens like in a dream. Those first few seconds stretch out like hours. But I don't hear the sounds of an explosion. I get up heavily, groping for the wall with my hands and leaning on it like a hundred-year-old woman. *Another wave.* My hands slip and I fall to the floor again. In parallel, I hear some new sounds. Only after a minute or seconds stretched out like clay I realize that these are my moans and incoherent words. *Fear, endless fear is rolling in with renewed vigor.* Only one thought beats in my head: *To the basement.*

Quickly. Right now. Immediately. The legs don't get into the jeans. My hands are shaking and can't zip up the jacket. The next wave of sound and overwhelming horror rolls too fast. *I didn't have time to prepare for this even mentally.* But still I find the strength to go to the window and see smoke nearby. At the exit of the apartment happens a loud explosion. Out of the corner of my mind, I realize that a rocket was shot down. *This has never happened so close before.* It doesn't end there. Soon the bastards make a third wave of missiles.

It was one of the most terrible days in my life. A few days later I feel a little better, but the stress hasn't gone away. There is a feeling of hopelessness that haunts me constantly.

269 Day of War

November 19, 2022

One of the few days that can be called *normal*. Normal means similar to life *"before"*. When you can lie in bed for a long time in your half day off, without urging yourself to do morning procedures, lazily read the news feed, comments in social networks and evaluate the number of "likes" which I received and call a friend *(Yes, there is also a connection and Internet!).*

The weather outside the window is not completely pleasing - snow-covered trees and still untrodden drifts of unusually blinding snow - *I do not like winter, and the cold scares me, but the alluring natural canvas awakens creative notes.*

Got sick. The feeling is not pleasant. But when there is such a rarity as the benefits of civilization, it becomes irrelevant. *Lemon, honey and warm tea will quickly fix the situation by tomorrow morning.*

Today there are no air alerts, which mean there is time to take a breath and improve my mental health. *A typical lazy, albeit working, Saturday afternoon.* We walk through the snowy VDNH. I pass by the familiar sprawling bushes, covered with a dense snow cover, and even for a moment there comes a feeling that everything is over, bad in the past.

I understand that this is self-deception, psychological self-defense, but thoughts make it a little warmer, despite the piercing wind and subzero temperatures. *Someday, one day, it will all end.* But the most important question is: *Will I see it? Will I witness the dawn of better times? Why do I need a world where I won't be? <u>Human life</u>* is the most valuable thing that exists in the world. *First - your life, the life of your relatives and friends, then - everything else.*

My priorities have always been different from the heroic-patriotic ones. *Eternity does not exist, the soul does not exist, there is only you, your personality and the present.*

In today's news, the feeling of incompleteness is more acute than ever. *By the end of the year, according to the forecast, we will return Crimea.* It sounds unrealistic, but it's nice. And at the same time, constant notes about the upcoming mobilization in orc-state are flashing.

I still don't understand how it is possible to defeat a country that is so outnumbered and which has been preparing for war for many years. At the same time, we have not yet received a sufficient number of offensive weapons. *For example, Himars missiles, which will be able to reach more cities of orc-state in response to attacks on our infrastructure.*

There are so many questions that deprive us of hope for a bright future.

P.S.: *Meanwhile, a strong explosion sounded near St. Petersburg.* The gas station is blazing. Sometimes it is useful to smoke in inappropriate places. It Burns Beautifully.

270 Day of War

November 20, 2022

Do you know what makes the life of a person, experiencing war, *different*? If we do not count the moments directly related to the fighting and any basic civilian deprivations - lack of electricity, water, heating or constant saving money, then these is memories.

You involuntarily compare your life *"before"* and *"after"*. It doesn't matter what you are doing at this moment - cooking porridge with a flashlight on, counting the minutes until the end of a planned power outage, trying to read a book by the weak light of a candle, or even enjoying such an unprecedented luxury as a shower, at that surprisingly pleasant moment when both electricity and water are present at the same time.

Your brains already perceive that nightmare, that deadly danger to which you are somehow exposed, being every new day in military operations taking place on the territory of your country, but the associative series works further... *What did I do exactly a year ago, on the 20th day of November?*

Surely, I was in a hurry to live another boring but effective working day. I was earning the new record cash profit and was drinking black coffee at this very minute, ordering sushi for the evening. I was interested in the goals that I set every subsequent day and was engaged in the implementation of new business ideas and projects. I wanted to achieve so much and earn "*all the money in the world*". But, as we can see, desire and perseverance were not enough. Everything disappeared into nowhere: money, projects, dreams, and self-development. Now I have only fear of each new day and the expectation of the worst times.

Do I regret not spending my time differently? I could travel more, work on my business less. But after listening to myself I understand that it was *my own way*. My main priority has always been earnings and self-development, which would allow me to see even more opportunities and realize more and more lofty goals and objectives.

My rather successful and promising life, which I created for myself, without outside help, was trampled by a *moth,* who fancied herself a king, and stupid orcs, who do not have their own opinions and blindly obey their head. And no matter how much time passes, their support does not fade, and their brains still do not start working. I do not know how a whole huge nation can be raised as slaves ready for slaughter and how to deprive the minimum skills of logical interconnection from birth.

But putin did it brilliantly. Bravo! 140 million degenerates, who believe that the Nazis "*bombed Bombas*" are nurtured, strengthened in the idea that they are defending their homeland on foreign land and saving russian-speakers.

You will not find such an incredibly stupid and senseless plot in any book.

I think about all this, while going to another city and absentmindedly looking at the snow-white landscapes outside the window. It's getting colder and sadder. The blackout is getting closer every day, and winter seems endless.

Arriving in another city, the last thing you expect is that the electricity will be turned off just at the moment, when you are drinking a cup of tea. Nevertheless, this happens more and more often, turning into a routine. But there is a positive side everywhere. Among the bonuses of living in the dark: *I'm getting better at cooking with a flashlight, I've almost stopped scattering salt on all surfaces, I can take not the worst photos with a contour lighting.*

P.S.: *From the good news from the outside, our guys have advanced in one of the most difficult areas - Zaporizhzhia*. We hold our fists and hope for the good. Berdyansk, I dream to see you free <3

271 Day of War

November 21, 2022

The weather today is perfect for the mood of millions of Ukrainians, which still stuck in February 24, 2022. Wet and dirty winter. Snow drifts melt intensively. Fog. Rain. Everything is very reminiscent of the imminent approach of spring. *Just like many others, I have been "stuck" in this one endlessly dragging event for 271 days. It's like a long, continuous nightmare that you fall into over and over again.*

We return home through unpleasant dampness and in the dark. The only illumination of the roads is the headlights of cars rushing towards. I observe strange flashes in the sky, similar to fireworks or air defense, but there are no alarms. A field, a deserted area, just a highway and a long road home.

Flashback: *flashes in my mind - 9 months ago, an endless road to the west, cars with frightened people stretching in long lines and <u>strange sounds chasing everywhere</u>*. Then it was impossible for an ordinary civilized person to understand what it was. Missile flight? Anti-aircraft guns? Artillery? Machine guns? Mortars? *You are going nowhere and the feeling that your life is completely destroyed at this very minute. You may never see your home again. And perhaps you will see, but not a house, but a funnel from it.*

On the morning of February 24, our everyday world, in which we comfortably existed, collapsed. The illusion that we will always be safe, we will be able to plan our lives and be its masters. My biggest illusion was that I thought I was surrounded by civilized neighbors, modern people who, like me, are outraged by the actions of their government and want to end this war as soon as possible. But it didn't happen.

Time after time, bumping into the complete detachment and indifference of people whom I considered *my friends*; I did not want to realize that it was not the events of the *so-called "SVO"* that affected them, but the fact that <u>they were like that before</u>. It just wasn't noticeable. More precisely, I didn't want to notice it myself.

When the world collapses around you, when <u>instead </u>of going to the cinema or cafe in the evening, you start thinking about *how to live the day tomorrow and how to find food in quickly emptying supermarkets* on cold February days; you begin to appreciate your past.

My cozy apartment, in which there was everything necessary for life and which was replaced by a dwelling of good hospitable people, but still according to their rules and principles; my financial possibilities, when there was no need to look at prices and save on anything; and also the usual benefits of civilization - light, heat, electricity, water, connection and internet. *Such mundane and simple things that are not available to me today, in the 21st century in sufficient quantity.*

Another day that had to be lived for some unknown reason is coming to an end. I've stopped looking for meaning in these things since the war started. One more day can be crossed out of life. *It was mostly dark, in the best traditions of blackout, and devoid of hope for the future.* I'm still sick and I don't feel better. I suspect that this is due to constant stressful situations. In previous years, my strong immunity allowed me to bypass colds and flu easily.

Mood: Linkin Park - In the end. It will all end someday, but not today.

273 Day of War, part 1

November 23, 2022

From today my cat is afraid of rockets.

My fearless cat, which always got into fights with his relatives and dogs of all sizes and stages of menace.

A cat, which climbed on the window at any sound to patrol the threat...

orc creatures broke her spirit, too. ~~Not just mine.~~

Today the day started almost perfectly. I spent yesterday in a fog illness. I don't remember what I did besides work and constant "*tea ceremonies*". But another day has been overcome and it's already good. This morning I felt much better and even slept well, despite the fact that there was a feeling that orcs had not showed themselves with new massive attacks for a long time ... And now, 8 days later, it started again.

The alarm in Ukraine spreads almost instantly, the map turns red. I barely had time to go to the shower and dry my hair when the flights in our direction began. Firstly they could not be heard. Only by monitoring the news every second, I read: *"The rocket is flying towards...", "The flight of 3 missiles was just seen a minute ago by...", "The work of air defense in the region"*. I can't say that it was scary at those moments, you get used to it.

Gradually. But when the rockets are whistling over your head again, when those terrible sound waves are heard once more and then piercing explosions, you get goosebumps from head to toe and the pain in your head begins to throb. *I survived two waves, like this one*, and on the third I was already in the corridor. The sounds are so loud, that the windows shake and it seems they are about to fly out.

It's cold in the corridor, but the sounds are quieter and the heart stops jumping out of the chest, although the body is still stretched like a string, and you listen to the sounds with tension and expectation of the worst. I don't remember how long I was in the hallway, half an hour or more, but when I heard one of the loudest explosions, I went to the basement at least.

It was very close and very scary. It was so scary that I wanted to run somewhere, disappear and vanish. But there wasn't any safe place. I have been feeling lately that I am in a trap from which there is no way out. We're stuck here until the end.

It is not surprising that this time even my cat could not feel herself as usual these nervous hours. She hid under the sofa and did not come out for hours. The cat turned out to be morally stronger than me. But even his psyche this time could not help but break down from such tension.

Now the temperature is back. *Disgusting state of health, mental and physical*. Stress is not good for anyone. There is no electricity, water, heating, connection, Internet. In short, nothing that could alleviate the effects of blows on morale. And it won't be for at least another day. Meanwhile, winter hasn't even come yet....

273 Day of War, part 2

November 23, 2022

My psyche is full of oddities that escalate during the war. For example, an acute desire to sit on the floor during an alarm. I understand that this is stupid, and that it will not help me in any way, but I continue to do it no matter what. And I feel better then. My psyche is *an unusual lady*, thinks it's safer this way. I've already come to terms with this point, and sometimes I let her unconsciously control my behavior.

Therefore, today I had breakfast with dumplings at 2 o'clock "in the morning" on the floor. I won't say that sitting on the floor on a cat scratching post is perfectly comfortable (~~not even close, the surface is wavy and hard~~), but at least it's not particularly cold. I drank tea in the same way. Cup - on a stack of work boxes and – Voila! With a strong desire, everything is possible.

Another oddity of mine appeared recently, during mass rocket launches, when for the first time more than 80 missiles were launched throughout Ukraine in several waves. *I began to mentally communicate with my good, but, of course, already ex-friend from orc-state*, who, for many years, was like a <u>brother </u>to me. *A brother in spirit, about whom I knew almost everything, and who always supported me*. I have even felt his support for some time since the war began.

Sincere friendship feelings, a desire to help from him, but at the same time complete passivity and lack of motivation to change anything with his own actions, like all others "good russians". Communication stopped suddenly. Because of strange questions; he lived in some other parallel reality.

Questions with positive intonation, like: *"By the way, have you seen any russian already? Haven't you met russkies in your city during the "special operation"?* My answer in the form of: *"Fortunately not, otherwise I would have already been dead or raped"* abruptly extinguished the desire to communicate further. There were several more attempts, but under the next strange questions and answers from *"my reality"* they always failed.

So, during the sounds of massive missile flights and explosions, I continue my conversation with my ex-friend mentally:

"How are you doing today?" Probably at this moment you go on a lunch break from work, see the next cats near your factory, take a photo and want to share them with me, but stop abruptly, remembering our last talk?

Perhaps you are experiencing discomfort and awkwardness that instead of the usual: *"Hello, aww, how sweet they are. I hope that soon you will have your own cat,"* you will get an answer: *"I'm sitting in the basement again. Missiles overhead. Your orc bastards are destroying us again. My life could end at any minute. Because of you too. After all, you keep paying fucking taxes that go to rockets that blow up everything around."* But you won't ask, and I won't answer.

After all, we haven't had anything to talk about for a long time. We are on opposite sides of the barricades. And this can't be changed.

P.S.: In the meantime, we are going to another area to contact our relatives. There is no connection anywhere. It is impossible to find out the news. Total darkness and huge traffic jams. 5 km per hour drive.

274 Day of War

November 24, 2022

The first full blackout in our country <u>began yesterday evening</u>. Before that, Kyiv, Odessa, Lviv, and Dnipro suffered after the orc attacks, but only partially and not for such a long time.

From more than 70 missiles and drones that the rashist creatures launched yesterday afternoon, 19 reached the targets. But it was enough to finish off our power system and plunge us into cold, darkness and take away from us the most necessary thing - *water*.

Still stunned after the close flights of rockets and explosions, we go to the city center.

You have to drive slowly, it is pitch darkness, not a single house is lit, and the only reflections are the headlights of cars, which also stretch in long and endless lines. There is no connection, absolutely, impossible to catch the mobile Internet, even with 3G connection. You have to drive up to the center to find out at least some news and contact your family and friends. And this in the current realities is about an hour's drive. On the way, we do not find a single working store or pharmacy. *It's like in the Middle Ages.*

On parking I read the news, in addition to the destruction and the human lives taken away by the orcs again, the government asks to remain calm and promises to return electricity by the end of the day. Sounds good. *But, of course, this does not happen.*

We return home, where there is no water, connection, electricity, Internet and wait for a miracle. *There are no miracles, so time passes incredibly long and boring.* I have 2 offline games on my phone, but it's impossible to play 7-8 hours in a row at the same time. Even bots get tired, dealing the same cards several times in a row.

Meanwhile, by 2 o'clock in the morning it starts to get cold. *Like a classic owl, I can't sleep. The whole atmosphere at home is also annoying.* You can't go to the shower; you can't read the news (*they warned about a new wave of missile strikes within the next hour. What if it's already started and catches me unexpectedly? I won't even hear a siren!),* you can't just at least read a book to calm down.

The cat fell asleep, burrowing between two pillows and stretching his hind legs under the blanket. Deciding to follow the example of the cat, I tried to get comfortable. *But sleeping in thermal underwear is not a big pleasure, it doesn't seem to be cold, but it's not comfortable either. Artificial fabric tightly wraps around the body and retains heat, but causes irritating sensations on my skin.* You are warm, but your face is unpleasantly cold from the temperature of the room outside.

I woke up every hour at night and checked phone connection, hoping to catch some news from Internet. *But alas*. In the morning, nothing has changed either. There is no opportunity to work and live, at maximum it can calls "*difficult survival*".

After long night and morning thoughts, I have decided to move for a while. I was tired, I wanted minimal human comfort. Under the sounds of loud cat howling, we got there an hour later. *We saw the light after 20+ hours of no electricity* (~~Though not for long~~, but being 6 hours with light today is a luxury). Experienced the pleasure of the presence of water in the tap (*Living with water is much easier and simpler, it's even better than electricity*).

At the moment, leaning back against a hot battery and having recently drunk a cup of black tea, I can say that *I feel myself like a human*.

Conclusion of the day: do not forget to enjoy the benefits of civilization. No one knows if you will be deprived of everything in one moment. Perhaps even, not only you, personally, but the whole country. As in our case.

277 Day of War

November 27, 2022

The previous days passed without incidents. With a countdown every 4 hours after 4 hours. *4 hours - you live like a civilized person - eat, drink, work, have fun, watching videos, and the next 4-5 hours you wait for the electricity, when you can come back to life again.*

We are slowly but surely getting used to the current conditions in a new city and in a new environment for us. Yes, there is always, at least, a connection and Internet, but the town, compared to Kiev, is small and inconvenient.

If the lights are turned off in our area, it automatically means that you will not be able to buy food in any store in the district. The same applies to pharmacies, banks and other establishments.

Meanwhile, winter is coming: already in the afternoon, the temperature is below zero, it is gloomy, chilly, often blows a cold icy wind and you feel nasty snow porridge underfoot. I want warmth... *And Victories*. It is the 10th month of this endless nightmare already, but you still can't just wake up.

As for my cat, which also moved in with us, she is in a better mood and situation than ours: *on the first evening she climbed all the corners, collected cobwebs wherever it possible, jumped on the TV three times and appreciated the number of shelves in the new apartment*. Every morning I wake up from the fact that someone with the *elegance of an elephant* cheerfully jumps from the bed to the bedside table, from the bedside table to the table, from the table to my hair. And so on for several approaches without a break.

About, probably, *the good news*: *I stopped being too picky and simple things began to please me*. After a few more or less quiet days, I get out of bed a little inspired and enjoy drinking coffee or waiting for electricity to drink it. I am pleased with the warmth of the batteries, which are nice to lean on while I'm sitting on the floor.

I am glad to have the opportunity to work quietly for a couple of hours without worrying that electricity will be lost. In recent days, business ideas have even appeared in my head and I want to implement them *right-at-this-very-minute*, which has not been happened since the very beginning of the war.

In the pre-war period, my life motto was development. It was interesting for me to gain new experience, to use more creative approaches even in the most familiar things, such as: simplify the cleaning process, add an unusual ingredient to borscht or complicate my daily workout with a more tricky exercise invented by me personally.

This is *my basic characteristic feature*, which sometimes manifests itself today as well. And yes, today is one of the most important days for me (*Oh, I am very modest and I have prepared the most interesting news for last*).

Today I am celebrating the day of the publication of my book on Amazon. Before that, I showed notes from this diary to my friends on the social network and many of them frantically recommended that I print it and make it available to others. Thanks to several people who helped me in getting information about the possibility of publishing a book and editing my annotation (**Moinak**, *hello and thank you very much!*), I did it. I can't say that with the publication of my diary, I'm waiting for something special. I don't wear pink-colored glasses and perceive reality as it really is. But if I manage to earn, at least, a couple of dollars, then I *will give all of money to Armed Forces of Ukraine*.

<u>Victory is the only thing that matters to each of us.</u>

278 Day of War

November 28, 2022

I've been having panic attacks for the last few days. *I couldn't sleep for a long time yesterday; I was lying, staring at the ceiling. My heart was pounding as if it was trying to jump out of my chest. It was difficult to breathe.* The condition always comes unexpectedly. You don't even seem to be thinking about anything, at least about something particular. And suddenly it happens. *In my case, this threatens not only acute panic, but also loss of consciousness.*

This has already happened this year, I have passed through it. I was returning from the bathroom to the bedroom and did not reach it. It caught up so abruptly and strongly that it darkened my eyes and made me sick. I remember that I reached the sofa, and then nothing... *Emptiness.* I woke up lying next to the sofa less than 30 cm away... So hard panic attacks began to torment me from the middle of summer. Before that, there was just a constant insurmountable fear that was getting stronger, then weaker.

Today was close to normal. There was even electricity almost all day. I worked, drank coffee, took a shower, calmly visited the shops I needed and bought groceries. *Such a quiet idyll with myself and the world around me lasted until the evening.*

The time was 22:02, when I overcame myself and decided to make this record. *Morale is very difficult.* I can't pull myself together, because there is not even an opportunity to drink a cup of tea with mint without light. We were warned that the biggest rocket attack since the beginning of the war is being prepared tomorrow.

For this attack orc-state will bring out 20 planes at the same time instead of the previous 11. It's scary, very scary and there is no end in sight. Even if we do not talk about the victims and destruction, everything is very bad, and it will be much worse. Already, people in many cities are sitting without light, heating and water for 20 hours a day, sometimes even more. Winter has not even officially begun yet, and the feeling of the end looms brighter and brighter.

There is no strength for optimism, to search for, at least, something positive. *It doesn't exist.* You just calm down a little, come to your senses after the previous week of shelling and it starts again.

Again, panic, despair, depression and all this at the same time. You are simply devoured and consumed by the feeling of hopelessness and the cage in which you are sitting. How to survive it? How to survive and not to become crazy? How to be sober and calm, knowing that tomorrow there will be another painful day and rockets flying overhead? *The only thing I realized is that neither meditation, nor soothing teas, nor medicines help in such a difficult time. All this makes you inhibited at best, but the feeling of inescapable horror remains with you always.*

I wanted to write about a lot of things today, but now only fear envelops me. There are no thoughts left, only a dead end. *Without hope for the best.*

279 Day of War

November 29, 2022

One of today's conversations with a barely familiar foreigner inspired me on some thoughts. Being an active user of the Hello Talk social network, which helps to learn and practice languages, I often meet people from other cultures and nationalities. Only a few are *aware* of what war is.

Basically everyone is asking: *"How is your working week? Did you have a good weekend?"* And they are sincerely surprised to hear in response that: *"Not so good, the war is going, you know."* This is followed by amazement, bewilderment and ridiculous questions, such as: *'Well, everything is not so bad there, is it? There are no military operations in your city, are there? Do you live as before?"*

Such questions are annoying and disgusting. Yes, we have a war, and it's been almost 10 months. No, there is not a single safe place in Ukraine. And, of course, Kyiv is one of the dangerous cities, where we live from attack to attack. And no, it is impossible to lead a normal lifestyle and work as before. The economy is destroyed; millions of Ukrainians with children have moved abroad; terrible unemployment situation. And there is no electricity for normal work.

In those rare moments when we have it here, you need to have time to do a *hundred-million-things-at-the-same-time.*

How to work? When to work? We're just surviving here. And the most difficult thing for our psyche is that we *realize* that it will not be better. Nothing will end at once. But we understand very clearly that it will be worse. *Much worse.*

Time after time, our energy infrastructure will be destroyed, then the gas infrastructure. And even if we survive from the missile attacks, and even if we are lucky and our homes are not destroyed yet, we will still survive in inhumane conditions until spring. No electricity, no water, no heating and, probably, no gas. And we won't even be able to earn our bread.

This is our reality. While residents of other countries choose gifts for Christmas, we buy canned food and snacks, tourist stoves and sleeping bags to survive in this hell. We do not live in dreams of the best; we know that it will not happen soon. At least, in the next 3-4 months.

It's sad when your cozy world collapses instantly. And it's even sadder to realize that the world will never be the same for you as it was before.

Last night I hardly slept again. Since the evening, I could not calm down after the news about the most large-scale attack. I wound myself up to a state of panic, remembering the horrors of last week. *Explosions overhead. The waves.* I lay for a long time with an internal tremor in my body, periodically glanced at the clock and read the news. I managed to get some sleep in 1.5 hours in the morning. The brains still turned off for a while. I woke up just in time to turn on the light and immediately got to work.

Several times there were large-scale alarms and fake news about launches. I drank sedative pills for the first time in six months, probably. But fortunately, there were no rockets overhead today and gradually, towards evening, I calmed down and even relaxed. The worst thing is that it will happen tomorrow, with a very high probability... Realizing this, it's hard to remain calm in the future.

I don't want to fall asleep to wake up in a new anxious day again. I just want to go back to the time, when you were not in mortal danger, when you could eat delicious food, relax under a movie after a working day, fall asleep...peacefully, knowing that tomorrow everything will be normal and predictable. Everything will be as it should be and you won't have to run to the basement and sit there for hours without connection, worrying that a new blackout will come or something will explode nearby *again*.

280 Day of War

November 30, 2022

A tedious, but effective day. +1 one book on Amazon today. It is a completely new experience, so glad I did it. I must say that everything new that I experience awakens in me an interest in life. I immediately want to start implementing another project as soon as possible and bring everything to life *right-at-this-very-minute*. And theoretically, it is even easier to *"infect"* me with profitable developments.

Recently I've been thinking about my positive qualities and came to interesting conclusions. I have no talents and nothing special that would distinguish me from others. But there is one trait that I have developed throughout my life - this is *purposefulness*. I am not afraid to try something new, I am happy to learn it and I definitely do what I started to the end, and often in a completely unrealistically short time. *I really love this feature of mine and I respect myself for it.*

It's easier for me than others to be consistent and persistent. I set a task - *to keep writing this diary*, for example - *and I keep it almost without interruptions, making stops only when it is unbearably difficult mentally*. In other moments, I do not give myself any slacks.

By the way, when you keep write a diary in which you sincerely share the main moments from life, without hiding your real self; it helps to *normalize the emotional component of life*. It becomes easier to experience the next day of the war, the moments of your life are better remembered, and now you are no longer living in a depressive routine, but trying to find both sides of today - *positive and negative*. And how after long conversations with a friend, it already seems that everything is not so bad.

Am I not ashamed to put my notes on public display, showing my real self? No, not at all. The life of millions of Ukrainians is now similar to mine, in many ways; it is a composite portrait of our nation, our way of life. Seeing how we live in these terrible conditions, you may begin to appreciate your life and your "*normal*" reality a little more. And, for sure, you can take something interesting for yourself; you will understand what we face every single day.

Today passed quietly. The electricity was on schedule, about 9 hours a day. This is a lot, believe me. I managed to work productively and finish another project. Today there have been many orders from my own online stores as well. Apparently, despite the war and the constant lack of basic conditions and resources, people wanted holidays. Many of them are coming soon (*Ukrainians celebrate St. Nicholas Day on December 19, and then the next holiday is January 1, New Year*), and they want to give their loved ones a good mood even despite the war.

There are a lot of rumors about Zaporizhzhia direction. Orcs are retreating to some settlements, deep into the occupied territory. *For example, today they left Mikhaylivka. And it seems that they plan to leave the Zaporizhzhia NPP.* But this is not accurate. Recently, it seems that our people have begun to respond to energy attacks, and now some regions of Belgorod and Kursk haven't electricity. *Meanwhile, we are still sitting in suspense, waiting for large-scale missile launches, which, according to experts, are about to begin. I wish it would stop already... at least weekly shelling with constant blackouts.*

I finish writing today's note at 23:52, November 30. And this means that winter will come in 8 minutes. *Ambivalent feelings.* There is definitely no joy, but there is some relief that we survived the autumn after all. I hope that this was the first and last military autumn. After this year it will be only peaceful and familiar seasons.

281 Day of War

December 1, 2022

Here is the first day of winter. *Officially.* In fact, we have absolutely winter weather since mid-November. *I've never liked cold and winter.* Previously, we were pleased with extra days off for the holidays, as I always worked 24/7. *And now I would be glad to fully immerse myself into work, but there is not much of it, and if I invent it for myself, then electricity does not allow me to realize my plans.*

There is, however, one activity that pleases me in winter. It is strange for choleric people, to which I belong to, but it is similar to meditation, calms the nerves and puts thoughts in order - *cleaning the car from snow*. Today I did it for a long time and with the special pleasure, despite the frost. But as a result, red frozen hands and a little moral relief. *Although, it's still sad all day.*

As soon as it snowed, *I remember February 24* and all the subsequent events. There were so many of them. Unexpected, shocking, stressful, intimidating. By the way, not only negative, some were also inspiring.

Since the beginning of the war, all Ukrainians have had a new vocabulary, their own national words, which we use every day.

We are amused by the common name - *"Chornobaivka"* (*Чорнобаївка*), associated with the stupidity of russians, who have long and persistently tried to storm it and always lost. We counted 20+ stupid attack attempts in which the orcs lost thousands of their soldiers and equipment. After that, until the end of the summer, the attempts continued: *the russkies again and again, like zombies, were going along the same road and, of course, died ... again.*

From the very first days of the war, an important word became: *"palyanitsa"* (*паляниця*), a type of Ukrainian bread, which only a real Ukrainian *can pronounce correctly*. The orcs have had so many attempts to pronounce it, but it never worked. So, this word has become the key, thanks to which unlucky masked rashists *can be easily recognized and exposed*.

We call russians by many of names: "*orcs*" (*орки*) - because they behave in a barbaric way, steal everything they see, including the most ordinary toilet bowls; "*rashists*" (*рашисти, derivative - fascists*), *raseyantsy* (*росіянці*), *rusnya* (*русня*). There are a lot of names given to this under-nation, these are some of the most popular (*I didn't write cursing words, censorship*).

Hlopok, bavovna (*хлопок, бавовна*) - it came to our lexicon from russian government. When we attacked russian cities, they called it "*hlopok*" (*or clap – closest word to English language*), because they did not want to send their population into a panic. "*Bavovna*" is a Ukrainian translation of the word "*hlopok*" with an accent on the first syllable. The joke had a big success and this word often uses even now.

Almost all foreigners, probably, heard the famous phrase: *"Russian warship go to ****"* or *"Good evening, we are from Ukraine."* Or the song that won the Eurovision Song Contest *"Stefania"*.

We also often use such national words as: *"kavun"* (кавун, *means – Kherson city*), *the ghost of Kyiv, Neptune, Bayraktar, Himars, blackout, Patron* (*the name of our most popular dog*). It seems that we will remember all these words for decades and be proud of our special "military" slang.

In the meantime, the war continues, and we are still facing long sleepless nights, hardships, "black" days and, deprived of any illumination, evenings. Will peace ever come? Although it seems impossibly far away, even at the 10th month of the war, but I understand that one day it will happen. *Will I ever be able to forgive the Russians for silence and lack of will?* No. Whether they are ex-friends or old acquaintances.

They are all equally to blame and silently continue to sponsor the terrorism of their country. There are no good russians, unless they are <u>200</u>. And every day their income and expenses help to kill our next civil people, destroy houses and our health.

282 Day of War

December 2, 2022

Another sad evening without electricity. It is absolutely dark in the apartment, but the windows of the houses opposite are lit. From a height of 4 floors, I watch how people live and wait to start living too. *There is still about 2.5 hours to wait*. Is it a lot or a little? If you endlessly look at the clock on your phone and remember about a thousand things that need to be *done-right-now-until-tomorrow*, then it feels infinitely long, if there is electricity in the house, then it's quite a bit. *Time stretches out when it's a winter night outside and there's nothing to do.*

I'm eating cutlets, which I have recently cooked (quite appetizing, I cook well), *but the taste of grandma's meatballs pops up so clearly on my tongue.* They are fatty, sweet and sour; enough big, made from freshly minced meat, from the best meat that my grandmother so scrupulously chose. A thick, attractive smell comes from the pan; you can't confuse it with anything. There are things that will never happen again. Even if it seems that they are eternal. *That they will always be like this.* Life is deceptive.

My grandmother was like a stronghold that should have always existed. She was in good health, looked younger, used cosmetics and kept positive in many things, even during her illnesses. *But it ended as if it had never happened.* Life stability is an illusion that ceases to exist at one moment. And then your usual world collapses, and you no longer realize whether you really exist or this is a long, endlessly continuing dream with no beginning and no end.

Next to the grandmother's saucepan, the outlines of the room appear. *Outside her window, I can feel the breath of the city of my childhood, where I haven't been since the beginning of the war (2014).* 8 years is a whole little life. During this time, the course of your thoughts changes, you grow and become a different individual, a different personality. *However, a part of you still remains in the past, turns your thoughts to what was.*

And now, I can already see my grandmother leaning towards me with a plate filled with meatballs. She smiles and says, "*Eat while they're hot. I'll bring you some more tea now.*" And this makes it unbearably painful, and at the same time warm. I remember. I still remember. Her expression, when she frowns, her grumpy, but, at the same time, loving voice, her slow, but firm pace. *It seems like it was only yesterday. But there is a gap between us. And this can't be returned.*

We used to live as if we are *immortal.* We often behave like robots; do not pay close attention to our loved ones, to their words and good actions. We exist day by day without full consciousness, forgetting that life is just a dash between two dates. There is only *today*, and tomorrow may be unattainable.

When you live in the mode of constant blackout and the absence of any good impressions, then all that you have with yourself are memories. I want to go back to the past, replay many moments, enjoy at least the last pre-war year. If we knew what this 2022 year would be like, we could change everything. Naturally, not the war, but our own life. *Make it happier and less stressful*, at least. At my enough young age, I already have a lot of gray hairs, and there are more and more of them. Mental health is a very important thing; your whole future life depends of it. Mine, unfortunately, has suffered a lot. And even when I'm feeling myself not bad and nothing terrible is happening around me, *I see rockets flying overhead every night*, I shudder and wake up.

Someday I may be able to restore my psychological state and regain calmness. But for that I need peace. *A peaceful sky and no orcs on our land*. ~~I hope~~ I'll see it. In the meantime, I meet the night of the next day near the window, watching the neighbors' glowing windows and dreaming of the simplest things: about electricity and Internet.

284 Day of War

December 4, 2022

Yesterday was a difficult day. ~~I didn't even have the strength to write anything about.~~ *We arrived in Kyiv,* in a cold apartment that was not heated for a week. It was so cold there, even in a jacket. I tried to keep warm in 3 pairs of socks and sneakers, but lost an unequal battle. *At a temperature of +10, it is unrealistic to stand or sit in a living room, just walk from corner to corner, blowing on your hands*. Although walking in 24 squares filled with boxes and goods is still a challenge.

Your life is going in a special way when you are deprived of connection, electricity, water and Internet at the same time. *The minutes seem to freeze*. You have absolutely nothing to do. You can't just sit - because it's too cold. You can't read the news and even find out about the air alert (*and yesterday it was, but I even didn't know about*), since you can't hear it at all here and the only way to understand about the danger without missiles flying overhead is to constantly view the news summary.

It seems that you are in a black hole, where everything is frozen in place, even time. During the day we had electricity - 3 hours and 20 minutes. That's all. It is impossible to heat the room in such an amount of time, but we tried anyway, and the maximum that we managed - *was to increase the temperature by 2-3 degrees for a couple of hours.*

Water is given according to the schedule, early in the morning and in the evening. And naturally, it often does not coincide at all with the supply of electricity. You can imagine taking a shower with such capabilities or washing dishes without catching a cold again. At 5 pm, they gave us electricity and it was almost possible to live *"normally"*, if you did not go far from the battery and drink hot tea all the time.

The *"quiet hour"* came at 10 pm. Firstly, electricity *"ran out"*, then water and within half an hour - Internet. Considering that I'm a classic owl, falling asleep so early is incredibly difficult. *I counted elephants up to 500 and have lost track, but I couldn't fall asleep for a long time.* Despite the fact that I was lying in a warm fleece jacket and pants with socks, it was cold and uncomfortable to lie down. The nose was cold, as were the ears. Only after 8 hours, the long-awaited electricity was given in the morning. *As soon as it turned on, I got to work and worked for the next 4 hours.*

I am writing this note, having returned to my mother, to her city. Compared to Kyiv, the conditions here are now at the highest level. *Although it's not even 11 pm yet, but my eyes are already closing. Relaxed. The long-awaited warmth.* You feel like a human, being here. I hope to wake up tomorrow without air alarms and rockets. I want to live quietly a little longer.

285 Day of War

December 5, 2022

Yesterday I couldn't sleep for a long time again, because of panic attacks. And today the worst thing, that I have imagined, _happened again_.

It's 14:52. I'm sitting on the floor as usual. The air alert is going already 1 hour and 45 minutes. *Another massive strike on all Ukraine for the reason to leave us completely without heating, water and electricity, which the orcs have been planning for almost 1.5 weeks.*

According to the media, the launch of about 150 missiles was planned today at 15:00.

But something happened that dramatically changed their plans.

For the first time in the history of the war, our drones were launched (most likely of our own production), which, having <u>overcome about 700 km</u>, hit the Engels base, where the russkies strategic bombers were located. 8 planes were unable to take off today, thanks to which they were able to launch much less missiles, than originally planned. Was it a one-time "promotion"? We really hope not. They should be responsible for attacks on our infrastructure and civilians. It helps to maintain our morale as well.

It seems that our air defenses are managing better with today's missiles. At least there is a lot of information about downed missiles. Infrastructure damages, of course, are happened too. Some areas are already without electricity again. But our people are trying and their actions are more and more successful.

To the accompaniment of the loud rumbling of my own stomach, I continue to monitor the news every second. The fear receded slightly. My legs are still shaking and I feel sick, but it is impossible to be afraid continuously even in such conditions. If everything ends well and we will have not a complete blackout, I dream of ordering sushi and eating them in a calm atmosphere. I can taste them right in my mouth. It's been so long since I've eaten them.

Now we have to save more and more, giving preference to simpler and calorific dishes, such as fried or boiled potatoes with cheese (*I like cheese in all dishes*) or soup, pasta, rice. But today, more than ever, I dream that the anxiety will end as soon as possible and arrange a little holiday for myself. I deserve it.

Meanwhile, as soon as I finished writing this message, the second wave of rocket launches began. It looks like I must to wait for a long time... If 1 wave lasted exactly 2 hours, then, by the same logic, there are still 4 hours to wait. Usually, there are 3 waves in a row follow one after the other and almost without interruptions.

It means, until 19 pm you will have to sit in the corridor, waiting and dreaming of the end of this. And after that there will be no water, electricity and heating, as usual. Tempting prospects.

The irony of fate also in the fact that all this time, after the last shelling, the whole of Ukraine has been living in a non-stop emergency shutdown mode and only from today it was planned to switch to planned ones, when the electricity will be 4 hours after 4 hours without it, not 2 hours after 8-10 hours without.

The air alert ended unexpectedly, at 16:30. I can't believe it. After large-scale attacks, the body usually relaxes instantly and immediately wants to sleep. But there are still a lot of things, which I must to do today. And of course, eat the sushi that I have already ordered.

286 Day of War

December 6, 2022

Today is a beautiful day according to my feelings. In the morning I feel satisfied with my life and productive. Today - no missiles according to all the laws of logic and common sense (*of course, it's hard to say about the logic and orcs in one sentence. The russkies, definitely, don't have it, but they also haven't missiles, prepared in sufficient quantities*). A quiet day that looms on the horizon is more than enough to feel happy.

I woke up at almost 9 am against my usual 10+. Only because of the huge amount of work, that was waiting for me. New projects, which I dive into with great pleasure (*I missed my work and finally see distant, but enough realistic prospects*), give me excitement and energy. I want to do everything; I want to surpass the plan for labor productivity, which I have developed.

Since my awakening, there was something else that gave me strength and positivity, which we can name as a clear <u>Turning Point in the War</u>.

If you remember, yesterday our side attacked orc fighter planes, which were at a distance of *600-800 km* from the unoccupied borders of Ukraine and attacked quite successfully, because these aircraft, carrying missiles on their wings to bomb Ukraine, will not take off in the near future.

Today it happened again. Now the drones have targeted the airfield in Kursk and the Bryansk region. In Kursk, it was blazing fantastically great. The explosion reminded the coming of a UFO. The ring of fire blazed beautifully, thanks to getting into the oil accumulator. *The orc side officially recognized the guilt of Ukrainian UAVs that were launched from our territory.*

So, at last that decisive moment comes and the war ceases to be one-sided, previously it practically did not touch the territory of Russia and only we suffered, without the opportunity to respond.

We are beginning to move into the phase of active demilitarization of this crazy pre-country. We clean it not only from orcs, but also from what harms us and can become an opportunity to attack other countries. This territory should be as disarmed and weakened as possible. This is the only way peace is possible. What happened must not happen again.

For all the wartime, I can highlight only a few very significant events for our side, such as: *the sinking of the cruiser Moscow, the destruction of the Crimean Bridge* and, finally, *attacks on airfields*. This is the most important signal that we are confidently going to <u>Win</u>.

Already, thanks to our drones, the russkies have failed to put the whole country back into full blackout. And it won't work anymore. Then there will be more - if our people continue their methodical attacks and destroy missile carriers, then our airspace will be much safer. The orc-state already has nothing to oppose in ground attacks.

Now the impression is beginning to form that everything can already end in the spring. There are more and more prerequisites for this and we are gradually beginning to be filled with hope for the best.

Its 20:41 and I've already done everything planned for today. I'm thinking of doing my tomorrow's tasks. Dark. *Another hour without electricity*. But there are a lot of ideas in my head and still a lot of strength to implement them. Therefore, sighing, I put down my phone and go to do them right now.

287 Day of War

December 7, 2022

Another day that I didn't notice. ~~Another day that can be just crossed out~~. But I'm even glad, it means that the time of winter and war has been reduced a little more.

The idea is increasingly coming to mind that with the spring warmth it will go to a logical end.

There is a big moral and physical fatigue from constant tension and stress.

Speaking of fatigue, I went to bed yesterday before it was even 12, because the body was just begging for rest after a busy working day. But in the end I slept for about half an hour and woke up with anxiety. *A large group of drones flew to Kiev.* After the announcement of the air alert, sleep was lifted quickly and easy.

Until 3 am, I frantically monitored the news and read how explosions were heard in the Dnipro, then in Zaporizhzhia. *And now, drones are already flying to Kyiv and flying over the Obukhiv district.* Naturally, fear and anxiety envelop. Drones are just as dangerous as missiles, although they have a smaller radius of destruction. And they are also flying very slowly, annoyingly buzzing.

Therefore, much more time passes in painful experiences than usual. They reach Kyiv only after 2 hours. *All this time I'm not sleeping and not even trying to do it*. I know it won't help. Everything, fortunately, works out, and ours shoot down absolutely all 16 drones, and the orcs left with nothing. It's a pity that my neurons don't recover from this. <u>But still I'm very proud of our Armed Forces of Ukraine</u>.

I fall asleep after 3 am, and wake up before 10 am. And again work, a huge desire to do as much as possible in a day. As a result, I do 3 times more than I planned, but I can't enjoy how cool I am. *Too tired for that :)* I found the time to write this note, when the clock is approaching midnight. I can't say that I'm unhappy with the day, but I just didn't notice it. Although, I am 100% sure, that this is a job for a good future. To feel any prospects for myself is vital for me, it gives me meaningfulness, strength and energy, and very important support for my psyche.

288 Day of War

December 8, 2022

The mood of today is *sadness*. Melancholy. New Year's holidays are approaching; I remember the cheerful bustle, preparation, and gift's purchases. Dreams... All this ordinary life has remained somewhere beyond the distant edge. It seems that all this was recently, but at the same time there is a feeling that in another life.

Those days it was especially pleasant to plan your future, make goals what to do for the next year, sum up the results of the outgoing. What can I say about the results of this year?

To be honest.

I became poorer, began to constantly count money and there was a feeling that I don't have it at all. Although, I'm trying to earn money with all my might. But inflation is huge. There is no electricity = no time to work, the demand for goods from people is decreasing. The economy, gaining speed, is rolling into the abyss. Saving money.

Every day, and it's annoying. Feeling not poor and being able to buy everything I want (at least, food and clothes) *was the most important thing* for me. Priority №1. Since I was born in the conditions of Donbass ghetto and tried at least at a conscious age to allow myself what I did not have in childhood. My family was so poor, that buying even a lollipop was an unacceptable luxury.

I *became nervous and got panic attacks*, from which I can even lose consciousness. Now it is much more difficult for me to control myself; and my morale is as hard as possible for all the time. Emotions like: from I want to die to a gloomy depression, when there is no strength even to get up. Full negative spectrum, without a hint of positive glimpses.

Decreased immunity. If earlier I was ill no more than a couple of times a year and not seriously, now I practically do not get out of painful states. Gray hair appeared, there are no physical forces that were before. Poor appetite and constant fatigue. The feeling that x2 became older in less than a year.

And the worst thing is, it seems that there will be a war for many more years. If so, how to survive? Does it make sense to suffer and why?

In general, an unpleasant result of the year. I can't find something positive in the whole year and I also can't tune in to positive emotions next year. Unfortunately, I don't have pink glasses like the others.

Although, sometimes I am pleased with the little things. I am glad that another damn day has passed, completely colorless gray and devoid of meaning. I am glad that on this day we sometimes had electricity and heating, and that we are still not forced to survive, but can lead an illusory visibility of life before. It is very illusory, which easily collides with reality, when you go outside and can't buy basic things in the supermarket, which closed during the day due to lack of electricity.

It's a basis! *The basis of your comfort.*

Today I was going to McDonald's for a cup of coffee and a burger, but I didn't wait for its opening. Even when the electricity was turned on, I waited for half an hour, but they didn't let me inside. *This is what the life of Ukrainians looks like today.* Except the nuances, when men are caught at roadblocks or in shops (*mainly in Western Ukraine*); where they are given summonses to the military enlistment office to die soon.

We realized that <u>our lives do not belong to us</u> for a long time, we "owe" from everywhere: to the motherland, to the government, to anyone, but not to ourselves, in order to live happily ever after. If you don't want to fight, you will go to prison, if you want to leave the country to find some kind of work, you will still stay here, without money and opportunities to change something, you will wait for your turn to die for the territories.

I will never understand and accept it. And also the fact that before the war, knowing absolutely for sure that it would soon begin, no one warned civilian people about it and did not give the opportunity to leave dangerous zones.

Many could have survived. The ones, whose are no longer there. Who remained forever torn to pieces in Bucha or burned alive in Mariupol. Of course, I understand and realize who/what was the main cause of the war and why it happened. But the fact remains, your life is nothing, no one appreciates it. It's just a bargaining chip. And so it will always be. It is difficult and hard to live with this truth. But I'm sure this applies not only to us, but also to more civilized countries, people in which, fortunately, have not yet had a chance to check it.

289 Day of War

December 9, 2022

It's finally possible to cross out one more day from my worthless life, and I'm glad of it. ~~Minus another boring, eventless day. Which you just want to forget and not remember~~. The only "event" is to go once again at McDonald's, which was closed. Electricity was turned off, when I was going down the steps of the entrance.

Even such a small thing as buying coffee somewhere in a street cafe is something incredible here. How good it was before, when everything depended only on you and your plans. *Now there is nothing left of the past life: no goals, no money, not even the opportunity to go somewhere.*

Walking through the dark streets, in the fog. Snow is falling or already lying, preparing to melt - that's all the variety. It's disgusting, it's dark around, and all shops are closed. Outside and inside, there is no hope for something bright and good.

The weekend is coming up. *What's the difference?* Except for the day of the week, there are no changes. There is nowhere to go, nothing to do, the last meaning is lost. Again the question: "*To live for what*?" The mechanisms of survival are still working, but you can't get the questions out of your head, they are enveloping your brains more and more tightly.

I'm terribly tired of everything. It would be nice to open your eyes and at least see the green grass around you, and not a solid dirty-white mess. You wake up and have a hard time fulfilling your basic needs by half *(there is no warm water to take a shower, there is no way to warm food and make coffee when there is no electricity, Internet doesn't work good, when you need to work and all this turns into daily torture)*.

Over and over again. *Just restrictions, no opportunities.* And endless fatigue from monotony; constant life with a flashlight and without satisfying your basic needs.

I've been thinking about the cinema all day today. I really want to go to the movies. An impossible and unattainable desire. *But the Avatar is released tomorrow*. Feeling sad...

290 Day of War

December 10, 2022

Another "round" number of the war. We are confidently reaching 300 day. Soon it will be 365 days – the full year... The war is only getting worse every day. I ask myself the question: *"Can't it just get worse all the time? When will be, at least, not a black, but a gray stripe?*

In the meantime, from the news for today, Odessa and the region remain completely without electricity. Restoration can take months ... they continue to shorten the time of electricity, wherever possible: Ivano-Frankivsk, Kyiv, Lviv, Zakarpattya. There have been no attacks here recently.

The weather has improved to +5-7, tomorrow it will be +12, but the situation with electricity continues to deteriorate sharply. If in Lviv now electricity is given 2-3 hours after 6-8 hours without it, then in many other cities there is electricity for a maximum of a couple of hours per day. *Where are we going? It's scary to imagine.*

In total cold and pitch darkness. Better to live in real Hell. At least, it's hot there.

It's 22:19. It is the third hour without electricity. I've done everything I can: I worked, took a walk in a foggy night with rare flashes of lights, worked out training. I sit and look at my watch stupidly. "*Real*" life will begin only in 1.5-2 hours. Weekend. The Internet barely loads. And I would like to watch the long-awaited series "*Wednesday*", advertised by everyone and everywhere. But it's impossible. Even some mini-video on YouTube won't load right now.

So I'm just sitting on the floor, with a warm battery behind me, the only one of the few benefits of civilization available at the moment. So many great ideas arise when you sit in the dark without electricity, and so few of them you have time to implement when it appears. Anyway, life, or rather its semblance, is still going on.

Today I can cross out another day with relief. ~~Minus another day of cold winter "hell" with a taste of war~~. Tomorrow will not be easier, but it will be possible to cross out one more day. *This is what I live for.* Life is beautiful, but I'm not sure about it :)

292 Day of War

December 12, 2022

Yesterday was spring weather. Such unusual and pleasant weather for our region ... +11. Rain, gusty, but not freezing wind. Pleasant spring smells of freshness and hope.

Today this fairy tale is over. Forecasters promised +5, but it was, in the best way, -2. There was no trace of the spring breath left. Yesterday the roads were absolutely clean, the ground was visible and green grass flashed in some places, and already a lot of snow had fallen overnight. It froze and everything went back to "*normal*".

I would like spring to come as soon as possible. *I'm tired of this cold weather, darkness, expectation for a complete blackout and gloomy forecasts. If it was February now, it would be much easier morally.*

15:30 - It's already dark here. The day light ended so quickly, but the worst thing is you can't just turn on the lights in your house. In a very good case, we have electricity 4 hours after 4 without. Today it was already turned it off at least twice: from 00:00 to 04:00 and from 09:00 to almost 13:00. The next portion of "joy" will be from 16:00 to 20:00.

When it gets dark outside you can only move around the house with a flashlight or candle. All simple household chores become more complicated in that time. Try to wash the dishes in the dark or cook a meal. Although I don't cook food when it's dark - I'm just waiting for the light to eat or drink tea, everything is on electricity (electric stoves, microwave etc.).

Again, there is a lot of talk about massive shelling. I want to live quietly for another week, at least. But, it seems, not in this reality. The orcs must fulfill their goal and leave us till New Year and St. Nicholas Day without the minimum benefits of civilization.

Only recently I have realized and accepted the fact that there is a ~~country~~ orc-state next to us, God forgive me, who's "~~people~~" scums hate all of us and me in particular, just because I was born and live here. And they wish me dead. If not 140 million of them, then, at least, 120 for sure. Inexplicable hatred even from my relatives.

Not to mention ex-friends and acquaintances. *How did it happen so quickly and at the same time?*

I don't understand, it's just some kind of zombie apocalypse, but I'm starting to accept it. These are the enemies. And even if the war ends ~~well for us~~... Although, this is not the right word, considering that many of our cities have been destroyed. Thousands of civilians were killed. Thousands of soldiers. And our whole nation, one way or another, suffered morally from the war. Our health deteriorated, panic attacks began, we aged this year as we could not have aged in the next few.

It is impossible to turn everything back, at least with our current generations. Almost until the end of the summer, my hatred of the russkies was periodic. *I started to hate them fiercely* when I found out info about Bucha and Irpen; when they killed us, ordinary people, in shopping malls, bombed hospitals and schools, when they wrote about it in the comments and rejoiced. But then it passed and sometimes I even wanted to talk to old friends, remembering our common topics, find out how their life is going.

For a very long time, I associated this war mainly with Putin and a small percentage of inadequate. *Understanding has come, when an important person from orc-state showed his true attitude to what was happening. The indifference, bewilderment, and absolute lack of comprehension that he demonstrated, began to open my eyes to reality. Even if he doesn't understand these simple things, what can I say about others?*

When the targeted attacks on infrastructure began and it became finally clear that the orc plan was to genocide of Ukrainians, my hatred became strong and constant. Now it's not changing, it's just growing and getting stronger. I want all of them, absolutely all of them, to suffer the same way we do. They don't deserve to be left out. I don't feel sorry for either adults or children. This nation no longer deserves to live a normal life.

294 Day of War

December 14, 2022

Yesterday I started translating my diary into English and realized that it will be more difficult than it seemed at first. Many phrases have to be rewritten again and in other words. *Oh, these difficulties of translation.* I still have half a month before the deadline; add an introductory word, make a layout and send it for verification. *It will be difficult, but I've been used to deadlines for a long time.* At the same time, I'm working in my stores, during the hot season and trying to do another project.

Now you can completely imagine how I live and work almost without interruptions. The periodic absence of light and connection gives peppercorn to my daily work. I'm not complaining, moreover, I like to work in difficult conditions, because in this case I only think about what I have planned, and not how tired I am of this tasteless and monotonous military life.

Speaking of monotonous... This morning wasn't even close. I woke up from air alert. And for the first time it was not an alert from the messages of the telegram channels, but the real one, nauseating and penetrating. For the first time in +- half a year, I heard it again. And if earlier I thought it was better to hear sirens in order to be aware of the danger, now I realized that staying in pleasant ignorance of the situation is less traumatic for me. *These sounds are so annoying and loud...*

As it turned out, the alarm was not false. 13 drones in two waves flew to Kyiv. This is not the first or second such attack. But there was something strange and unusual about all this. Drones always fly to our region from the Black Sea and do it very slowly (2-3 hours to Kyiv, at the same time they buzz violently, it is impossible not to wake up from this), which means that they are forced to fly one way or another several areas until they reach our territory. The air alert is usually activated from the moment they are launched and starts from the Kherson or Mykolaiv region, and then quickly spreads as they move deeper into the country.

This time, sirens were given only in Kyiv and 2 nearest regions. *And almost immediately after that*, the work of air defense already in our region followed. *This means that the drones in some strange way flew through half the country, moreover, very slowly and were noticed only on approach*. It doesn't sound encouraging at all. But whatever it was, all of them were fortunately shot down, although several houses were partially destroyed. But, at least, without casualties and without hitting the infrastructure.

I'm writing this at 18:56. It is pitch darkness here. Under the straining sounds of our aviation. We're catching drones again. Aviation flies very fast and noisy, even with the music on, I hear it over and over again. A difficult evening. There is no Internet, I'm dreaming of warm tea and cheesecakes.

About the good news, I have already ordered gifts for all my important people for Nicholas Day, which is celebrated in Ukraine. On this day, gifts are given to adults and children, usually a Christmas tree is installed by this time as well and the house is gleaming with bright decor.

By the morning of December 19, children are enthusiastically looking for gifts under the pillows and adults, with smiles, checking their boots for funny souvenirs in them. By the way, today I have ordered the last gift for Nicholas Day - to my friend. *And even if she is in Lviv now, and I can't to hide this beautiful gift set of pastries in her shoes, I think she will still be pleased to receive it by the post-service :)*

296 Day of War

December 16, 2022

It is a very difficult and morally oppressive evening. Probably one of the hardest, since the beginning of the war. There is complete devastation, disappointment and expectation of even greater intensity of hostilities.

There were a lot of bad events today. But I'll start telling you about the day from the end.

Late evening. 23:00. Now we are sitting and talking about experts and opinions about what is happening from the government (VH interview with Zaluzhnyy).

The basic result: everything sucks.

In January-February, will be a *large-scale offensive on Kyiv*. Again. Maybe russia + belarus, maybe only orcs. But the forecasts are serious and it will happen again. If you're lucky, then in the spring, but intelligence data shows the probability of this already at the beginning of the next year. Then there will definitely be *Iranian ballistic missiles*. The orc-state has signed a contract with Iran. When? No one knows. Most likely it will coincide with a new offensive on Kyiv.

There will be also *a large-scale mobilization of orcs* soon. To sum up, the worst is ahead. And it will be much worse than what was expected. The balloon of hope burst, barely filled. I don't believe in victory, I don't believe in the best, I don't believe that something good is ahead. What kind of victory can there be if I may not be there. I want it to be over. I just want to live and not be afraid for my life every day, every morning.

This morning was terrible. I slept tight until 9 am. I met my mother in the kitchen to get the next news about the large-scale alarm in Ukraine. *Scaring. This fear does not disappear anymore, it seems to have become a part of me and is constantly bursting out.*

Explosions were heard, infrastructure was damaged. There was no electricity, water, heating, connection and Internet. 40 missiles were launched only to Kyiv. The largest attack on Kyiv since the beginning of the war. The wreckage of one of the missiles hit the neighboring residential complex. When death is near, and you realize it, you especially want to live. At least, a little more. I'm only 30. And I understand that I didn't see anything, but a permanent job. *Very depressive mood. There is no strength for anything.*

I'm so tired of all this. Why wasn't I born in another country? Why don't my moral principles allow me to drop everything and leave to save my life? I can get a job and live anywhere, just not to hear explosions, not to be afraid of… How simple and at the same time difficult it is to hold on to your life. In which there is nothing good left, only the survival instinct, but it continues to work…

298 Day of War

December 18, 2022

It was 2 completely good and normal days. For a while, I forgot that it was a war, and it seemed that today was an ordinary weekend after difficult working days in the hot season.

Yesterday afternoon we returned to Kyiv. For all the time we got electricity only for an hour before going to bed. It was difficult, include the fact, that the apartment was not heated for 3 weeks and the maximum temperature in the room was +10. But generally it wasn't so bad. We slept in sleeping bags, (the good thing that we have it). The evening was pleasant and memorable.

We finally watched to Avatar 2, which I've been waiting for almost 13 years after the release of the first part. I can't say that I liked the movie. Something more unusual was expected than a rather banal plot, built on a sentimental home theme, but it was nice to go to the cinema after so many months. *Really nice.*

From the movie, for me, the analogy with the orcs was clearly traced. People from their planet behaved exactly like our orcs: they barbarically destroyed all living things and used merciless violence against the indigenous inhabitants of the planet.

I don't know if you noticed that their combat vehicles had a 'V' sign on them, exactly the same as our orc-state neighbors have. A coincidence? I don't think so ☺ I appreciated this moment. I hope the end of our orcs will be sad and fast, like in this movie.

After the movie, it was nice to visit our favorite cafe and eat the usual portion of

Asian pasta with chicken. It's just like the good old days. Nostalgia… *Maybe these times will come back?* I want to believe…

Returning home, I noticed that the whole of Kyiv was unusually glowing, just like before the destruction of our infrastructure: lights around, houses, commercial buildings. Incredible beauty... Real pleasure to look with a smile. Song: *"The day will come, when the war will end"* («Настане день, коли закінчиться війна) was the leitmotif of my evening. I listened to her over and over again.

It's 21:26, Sunday evening. The day passed very quickly and unnoticed. It is insanely joyful to return home at least for a while: take a great hot shower, relax in the foam bath, drink coffee from your favorite mug, see the familiar landscape in the window, and visit your favorite cafe with the perfect black coffee. *These things can make you happy to tears when there is a war in your country. You become sentimental and sensitive. Even the smell of your perfume and soap can awaken this atypical emotional sensitivity.*

I'm sitting at my desk and admiring my "work of art" - *a painting of the burning Kremlin*, which I had painted by numbers. It looks quite well. The most inspiring feeling, <u>when Moscow is burning</u>.

299 Day of War

December 19, 2022

Time 19:41. I haven't any energy to live. I'm feeling only fatigue and disgust of life. I'm trying to recover from last night. The weekend went so well and ended in a nightmare…

Last night I have planned to work slowly and finish all my tasks, but no miracle happened. At 22:30, an air alert was announced due to the launch of drones; and at 23 pm electricity was already turned off. Firstly, our Telegram channels said that there were few drones, only 15-16 shaheds and things were going well, because only in Mykolaiv region 10 of them were destroyed and a few more in the following areas.

I felt hope, that they would not reach Kyiv. And their goal is always Kyiv, but it didn't happen.

At the first explosions, I jumped out into the corridor. My previous experience immediately popped into my head: rocket launches, waves over the house, shaking windows, incredibly loud explosions over and over again, and all this in minimal proximity to you... It's cold and uncomfortable in the hallway; I squatted down and leaned on the wall. *It's impossible to sit like this for a long time, my legs are shaking, my heart is jumping out of my chest; I'm feeling sick and wanting to cry. I'm so tired of everything.*

I sat for half an hour, listening to the sounds. It seems to have become quieter, although the alarm continued and at least 3 hours had passed since its beginning. I came home in the dark. Electricity didn't come back. I took off my jacket blindly and threw it in the hallway. I tried to cover myself with a sleeping bag to warm up a little and calm down. It helped not much, my body continued to shake periodically.

The series of explosions is closer and louder. I'm jumping up and starting to breathe heavily. *Moans or loud breathing?* I don't understand it. But these sounds are going from me. It doesn't matter now. *Hatred is boiling, fear is piercing and acute pity for myself, my negligible life*. Reading the news. Shaheds over Kyiv. They are flying to the left bank of river. *A large group.*

If it's on the left, then everything is not so bad, then I won't hear any more explosions, I persuade myself and try to control the emotions. It doesn't work.

Another wave. A loud explosion. I understand that the drone was knocked. Very loud again. A minute later I'm back in the hallway. Legs do not go, trembling all over the body. *I'm listening to the sounds. Catching echoes of aviation, the work of air defense.*

A few more hours passed like that. Sometimes I sit in the hallway and then come back and squat at the front door. Air alerts have already been canceled in all regions, except Kyiv. When here? I want to sleep so much, despite the increasing fear. But the drones keep flying and flying. I read about it in the news every minute and hear explosions - muffled and rolling, distant and close. I hear the downing of drones.

Endlessly over and over again. So the morning came. It's 5 am and I haven't slept for half an hour. Only at 5:20 the air alert was cancelled and after 10 minutes announced again, about which, fortunately, I didn't know, because at this time I forget myself in a weak anxious sleep. I can hear the sounds of distant explosions through my sleep, but I didn't care anymore. I didn't have the strength to get up. There is no strength to be afraid again.

I wake up around 11 am from the fact, that it's terribly cold even in a sleeping bag. At night it was -8 and the temperature in the house does not seem to exceed +6-7. There is no electricity, connection and Internet. Just water. Therefore, I will find out about the energy infrastructure hitting, the victims among the civilian and destruction of 8 residential buildings. We drive 40 minutes to the city center to catch at least some Internet and process the orders.

By the evening I managed to get some sleep and now I'm gradually getting myself in order. I make coffee and get ready to work for the next few hours. *We need to survive further.*

Printed in Great Britain
by Amazon

32626057R00059